I0803878

KARFL HUSA

AL FRESCO

for Concert Band

(full score)

AMP 7451

ISBN No. 978-0-6340-1353-9

Associated Music Publishers, Inc.

DISTRIBUTED BY
HAL•LEONARD® CORPORATION
7777 W. BLUEMOUND RD. P.O. BOX 13819 MILWAUKEE, WI 53213

ITHACA COLLEGE
Walter Beeler
Memorial Commission Series

Al Fresco by Karel Husa is the first of a series of original band compositions commissioned by the many people who have been influenced by Walter Beeler, "Mr. Band" at Ithaca College for over 40 years.

Upon his retirement as director of the noted Ithaca College Concert Band in 1968, alumni, students, faculty, and friends, as well as music publishers and manufacturers, began this project as a tribute to the man who accomplished so much for the bands of America.

FOREWORD

Al Fresco has no programmatic content. However, the title indicates my admiration for the art of painting, especially mural painting on wet plaster. And I have always been greatly moved by the forceful, even grandiose and rough, mysterious pictures dealing with primitive life, war, and pageantry.

The composition has been commissioned for the Ithaca College Concert Band as the first of the Walter Beeler Memorial Commission Series. The first performance was given by the Ithaca College Concert Band (Edward Gobrecht, director) at the MENC Convention in Philadelphia on April 19, 1975 with the composer as guest conductor.

This work is intended to be performed by young, high school musicians. Some of the passages in mm. 219–238 may seem difficult and, although pitches and rhythms are written out, they do not need to be played exactly. The performers are given freedom in expressing the ascending as well as descending lines and may perform the speed of the rhythmic figures according to their abilities. The conductor may be helpful in suggesting easier possibilities. Also, it is necessary that the conductor clearly indicate tempi of mm. 235, 236, and 239, so that all those who are playing the *ad lib.* passages can enter again in the tempi of the strict measures.

—Karel Husa

 = highest possible note (indefinite pitch)

 = lowest possible note (indefinite pitch)

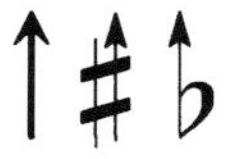 = quarter tone up

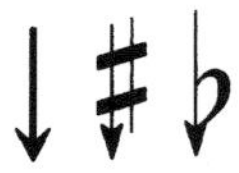 = quarter tone down

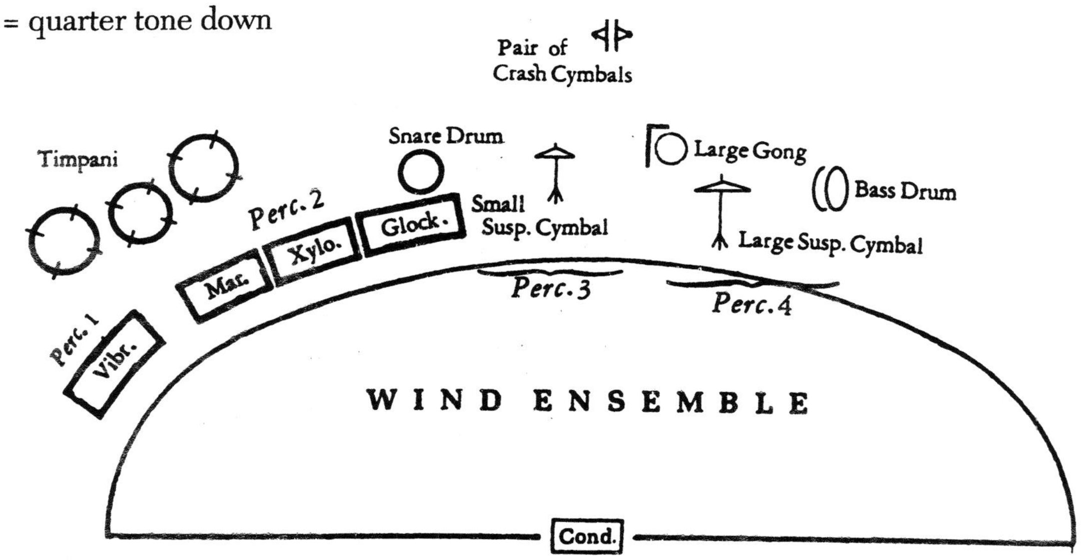

Distribution of Instruments

KAREL HUSA

AL FRESCO

for Concert Band

(full score)

Associated Music Publishers, Inc.

DISTRIBUTED BY
HAL•LEONARD®

Instrumentation

Piccolo
2 Flutes
2 Oboes
English Horn in F
3 Clarinets in B♭
E♭ Alto Clarinet
B♭ Bass Clarinet
2 Bassoons
Contrabassoon

2 Alto Saxophones in E♭
Tenor Saxophone in B♭
Baritone Saxophone in E♭
Bass Saxophone in B♭ and Contrabass Clarinet in B♭

4 Trumpets 1 in B♭
4 Horns in F
3 Trombones
Baritone
Tuba
String Bass (preferably 3–4 players)

Timpani
Percussion (4 players):
1. Vibraphone
2. Glockenspiel, Xylophone, Marimba
3. Glockenspiel, Large Crash Cymbals, Small Suspended Cymbal, Snare Drum
4. Large Crash Cymbals, Large Suspended Cymbal, Large Gong, Bass Drum

Piano (completely open or with the cover removed)

duration: ca. 12 minutes

A complete set of parts is available for purchase, order no. 50244600

AL FRESCO

Karel Husa

Picc.
Fl.
Ob.
E. H.
E♭ Cl.
B♭ Cl.
A. Cl.
B. Cl.
Bn.
A. Sax.
T. Sax.
Bar. Sax.
Bass Sax.
Cb. Cl.
Tpt.
Hn.
Tbn.
Bar.
Tba.
Str. B.
Cbn.
Timp.
Mar.
Piano
10
15
Solo
echo tone
gliss.
gl.
pppp
pp
no vibr.
ppp
perd.
Harmon mute
sempre

20
Picc.
Fl. 1 2
a2
warm sound
fp
Ob. 1 2
1.
1. non. vibr.
pp cresc.
mp
E. H.
E♭ Cl.
pp non. cresc.
perd.
(Solo)
Tutti
ppp
B♭ Cl. 1 2 3
A. Cl.
B. Cl.
Bn. 1 2
A. Sax. 1 2
T. Sax.
Bar. Sax.
Bass Sax. Cb. Cl.
Str. (fiber) mute
Solo
Tpt. 1 2 3 4
1. mute
3. mute
2. mute
4. mute
Hn. 1 2 3 4
Tbn. 1 2 3
Bar. 1 2
Tba.
Str. B. Cbn.
Timp.
Suspended Cymbal, on the dome
Perc.
L.V.
Vibraphone
normal (medium) mallets
Vibr.
Mar.
bring out
Piano

25
Picc.
Fl. 1 2
Ob. 1 2
E. H.
E♭Cl.
B♭Cl. 1 2 3
A. Cl.
B. Cl.
Bn. 1 2
A. Sax. 1 2
T. Sax.
Bar. Sax.
Bass Sax. Cb. Cl.
Tpt. 1 2 3 4
Hn. 1 2 3 4
Tbn. 1 2 3
Bar. 1 2
Tba.
Str. B. Cbn.
Timp.
Perc.
Vibr.
Mar.
Piano
pp
p
mp
mf
dim.
Solo
echo tone
Cb. Cl.
1. Solo
p ma espressivo
Harmon, stem off
fastest flutter
pp non. cresc.
cresc.
Straight mute
Solo (mute)
in the middle
Sus. Cym. on the
G.
fp
cresc. poco a poco
inside, with nail
L.V.
on keyboard

30
35
Picc.
Fl. 1 2
Ob. 1 2
E. H.
E♭ Cl.
B♭ Cl. 1 2 3
A. Cl.
B. Cl.
Bn. 1 2
A. Sax. 1 2
T. Sax.
Bar. Sax.
Bass Sax. Cb. Cl.
Tpt. 1 2 3 4
Hn. 1 2 3 4
Tbn. 1 2 3
Bar. 1 2
Tba.
Str. B. Cbn.
Timp.
Perc.
Vibr.
Mar.
Piano
a2
1. Solo
perd.
ad lib.
2. Soli
echo tone
dim. poco a poco
perd. ad lib.
Solo, echo tone
pp echo tone
dim.
poco a poco
poco à poco
Harmon, stem off
fastest flutter
Solo
non. cresc.
Tutti
Straight mute
gliss.
edge
poco cresc.
Glockenspiel
molto cresc.
medium mallets
cresc.

Allegro risoluto
40
Picc.
Fl. 1 2
Ob. 1 2
E. H.
E♭ Cl.
Tutti
B♭ Cl. 1 2 3
A. Cl.
B. Cl.
a2
Bn. 1 2
A. Sax. 1 2
T. Sax.
Bar. Sax.
Bass Sax. Cb. Cl.
Allegro risoluto
40
Tutti open
Tpt. 1 2 3 4
a2 open
Hn. 1 2 3 4
open
Tbn. 1 2 3
a2
Bar. 1 2
Tutti
Tba.
Str. B. Cbn.
Timp.
S.D. snares off
Perc.
B. D.
"black" keys
Vibr.
"white" keys
gliss.
Piano

*ad lib. 1st beat

50
Picc.
Fl.
Ob.
E. H.
E♭ Cl.
B♭ Cl.
A. Cl.
B. Cl.
Bn.
A. Sax.
T. Sax.
Bar. Sax.
Bass Sax. Cb. Cl.
Tpt.
Hn.
Tbn.
Bar.
Tba.
Str. B. Cbn.
Timp.
Perc.
Vibr.
Piano
a2
ad lib.
Harmon, stem in
Sus. Cym.
Sus. Cyms.
S. D.

55
60
Picc.
Fl. 1 2
Ob. 1 2
E. H.
E♭ Cl.
B♭ Cl. 1 2 3
A. Cl.
B. Cl.
Bn. 1 2
A. Sax. 1 2
T. Sax.
Bar. Sax.
Bass Sax. Cb. Cl.
Tpt. 1 2 3 4
Hn. 1 2 3 4
Tbn. 1 2 3
Bar. 1 2
Tba.
Str. B. Cbn.
Timp.
Perc.
Vibr.
Mar.
Piano
p espr.
p cresc.
Solo
Tutti
cresc. poco a poco
Harmon, stem in
(4.)
p espr.
Str. Bass
Sus. Cym. Wooden stick
hard mallets
sim. stacc.
sf
mp
fp

Picc.
Fl. 1 2
Ob. 1 2
E. H.
E♭ Cl.
B♭ Cl. 1 2 3
A. Cl.
B. Cl.
Bn. 1 2
A. Sax. 1 2
T. Sax.
Bar. Sax.
Bass Sax. Cb. Cl.
Tpt. 1 2 3 4
Hn. 1 2 3 4
Tbn. 1 2 3
Bar. 1 2
Tba.
Str. B. Cbn.
Timp.
Perc.
Vibr.
Mar.
Piano
cresc. poco a poco
65
mp
f
a2
f espr.
open
Str.Bass.
cbn.
Cbn.
Bass Drum
hard mallets
ad lib.
sf

70
Picc.
Fl. 1 2
Ob. 1 2
a2
E. H.
E♭ Cl.
B♭ Cl. 1 2 3
sim.
A. Cl.
B. Cl.
Bn. 1 2
A. Sax. 1 2
T. Sax.
Bar. Sax.
Bass Sax. Cb. Cl.
Tpt. 1 2 3 4
open
Hn. 1 2 3 4
Tbn. 1 2 3
Bar. 1 2
Tba.
Cbn.
Str. B. Cbn.
Timp.
Perc.
Piano

75
Picc.
Fl. 1 2
Ob. 1 2
E. H.
E♭ Cl.
B♭ Cl. 1 2 3
A. Cl.
B. Cl.
Bn. 1 2
A. Sax. 1 2
T. Sax.
Bar. Sax.
Bass Sax. Cb. Cl.
Tpt. 1 2 3 4
Hn. 1 2 3 4
Tbn. 1 2 3
Bar. 1 2
Tba.
Str. B. Cbn.
Timp.
Perc.
Vibr.
Piano
f marc.
più f
sim.
a2
B.D.
p cresc.
2 Cyms.
Sn. D.
hard plastic mallets white
motor on
f gliss
secco

80
Picc.
p sub. cresc.
f fl. t. quasi gliss
Fl. 1 2
a2
p sub. cresc.
Ob. 1 2
a2
E. H.
E♭ Cl.
p sub. cresc.
(doubletonguing ad lib.)
½ step simile
B♭ Cl. 1 2 3
A. Cl.
B. Cl.
Bn. 1 2
A. Sax. 1 2
reedy, harsh
T. Sax.
Bar. Sax.
Bass Sax. Cb. Cl.
quasi glissando
fl. t.
Tpt. 1 2 3 4
sub. cresc.
Hn. 1 2 3 4
Tbn. 1 2 3
Bar. 1 2
Tba.
Str. B. Cbn.
Timp.
Sus. Cym.
cresc.
L. V.
Perc.
B.D.
S. D.
motor off
Vibr.
hard mallets
Mar.
sim.
Piano

85
90
Picc.
Fl. 1 2
Ob. 1 2
E. H.
E♭ Cl.
B♭ Cl. 1 2 3
A. Cl.
B. Cl.
Bn. 1 2
A. Sax. 1 2
T. Sax.
Bar. Sax.
Bass Sax. Cb. Cl.
Tpt. 1 2 3 4
Hn. 1 2 3 4
Tbn. 1 2 3
Bar. 1 2
Tba.
Str. B. Cbn.
Timp.
Perc.
Vibr.
Mar.
Piano
1.
p cantabile
dim. poco a poco
ff
dim. poco a
Str. fiber mute
fl. t. gliss.
ad lib
fl. t. (ad lib)
St.B
Cbn.
a2
St.B. pizz.
p ma sonoro
B. D.
soft mallets
medium mallets
sim.
plays only if string bass unavailable (until 1)

95
Picc.
Fl.
Ob.
E. H.
E♭ Cl.
B♭ Cl.
A. Cl.
B. Cl.
Bn.
Solo
A. Sax.
T. Sax.
Bar. Sax.
Bass Sax.
Cb. Cl.
Tpt.
Str. fiber mute
Hn.
stopped, brassy
Tbn.
Bar.
Tba.
Str. B.
Cbn.
Timp.
Perc.
Sus. Cym.
S. D.
Vibr.
Mar.
Piano

* Oboe 1 if no E. H.

110
Picc.
Fl. 1 2
Ob. 1 2
E. H.
E♭ Cl.
B♭ Cl. 1 2 3
A. Cl.
B. Cl.
Bn. 1 2
A. Sax. 1 2
T. Sax.
Bar. Sax.
Bass Sax. Cb. Cl.
dim.
tr
ppp
p
perd.
cresc.
110
Tpt. 1 2 3 4
Hn. 1 2 3 4
Tbn. 1 2 3
Bar. 1 2
Tba.
Str. B. Cbn.
Str.B.
arco
Cbn.
pizz.
Timp.
Perc.
Sus. Cym.
B.D.
S. D.
Vibr.
Mar.
Piano
(Ped.)

115
Picc.
Fl. 1 2
Ob. 1 2
E. H.
E♭ Cl.
B♭ Cl. 1 2 3
A. Cl.
B. Cl.
Bn. 1 2
A. Sax. 1 2
T. Sax.
Bar. Sax.
Bass Sax. Cb. Cl.
Tpt. 1 2 3 4
Hn. 1 2 3 4
Tbn. 1 2 3
Bar. 1 2
Tba.
Str. B. Cbn.
Timp.
Perc.
S. D.
Mar.
Piano
fl. t.
flutter t.
quasi gliss.
Tutti
a2
open
nat.
arco
cresc.
mp
mf
f
p

120
125
Picc.
Fl. 1 2
Ob. 1 2
E. H.
E♭ Cl.
B♭ Cl. 1 2 3
A. Cl.
B. Cl.
Bn. 1 2
A. Sax. 1 2
T. Sax.
Bar. Sax.
Bass Sax. Cb. Cl.
Tpt. 1 2 3 4
Hn. 1 2 3 4
Tbn. 1 2 3
Bar. 1 2
Tba.
Str. B. Cbn.
Timp.
Perc.
Mar.
Marimba player goes to Glockenspiel
Piano
a2

Picc.
Fl. 1 2
Ob. 1 2
E. H.
E♭ Cl.
B♭ Cl. 1 2 3
A. Cl.
B. Cl.
Bn. 1 2
A. Sax. 1 2
T. Sax.
Bar. Sax.
Bass Sax. Cb. Cl.
Tpt. 1 2 3 4
Hn. 1 2 3 4
Tbn. 1 2 3
Bar. 1 2
Tba.
Str. B. Cbn.
Timp.
Perc.
Vibr.
Piano
130
(W/o 1. solo)
a2
sim.
cresc.
1. and 3.
2. and 4.
Sus. Cym.
hard mallets
black & white ab lib.

* Alto and Bass Cls. may play ([ ]) if difficult for Bassoons.

* * If 2 Tubas divide as follows:

140
Picc.
p marc.
Fl. 1 2
2. Solo
E.H.
Ob. 1 2
E.H.
E♭ Cl.
B♭ Cl. 1 2 3
A. Cl.
B. Cl.
Bn. 1 2
A. Sax. 1 2
T. Sax.
Bar. Sax.
Bass Sax. Cb. Cl.
Straight metal mute
Solo
Tpt. 1 2 3 4
Straight metal mute
Solo
1. mute
3. mute
Hn. 1 2 3 4
open
Tbn. 1 2 3
Bar. 1 2
sim.
Tba.
Str. B. Cbn.
Timp.
2 Cyms.
Perc.
brass mallets
Glock.
medium mallets
ma sonoro
Vibr.
ma sonoro
Piano

145
Picc.
Fl.
Ob.
E. H.
E♭ Cl.
B♭ Cl.
naturale
naturale
A. Cl.
B. Cl.
Bn.
A. Sax.
cresc. poco a
T. Sax.
Bar. Sax.
Bass Sax.
Cb. Cl.
145
Tpt.
Straight metal mute
Hn.
mute
mute
cresc.
espr.
Tbn.
Bar.
Tba.
Str. B.
Cbn.
Cbn.
Timp.
Perc.
2 Cyms.
Glock.
Vibr.
Piano
espr.

150
Picc.
Fl.
Ob.
E. H.
E♭ Cl.
B♭ Cl.
A. Cl.
B. Cl.
Bn.
A. Sax.
T. Sax.
Bar. Sax.
Bass Sax. Cb. Cl.
Tpt.
Hn.
Tbn.
Bar.
Tba.
Str. B. Cbn.
Timp.
Perc.
Glock.
Vibr.
Piano
poco
a poco
cresc.
poco a
gliss.
a2
cresc. poco a poco
Straight metal mute
Tutti
(mutes)
2 Cyms.
Sus. Cym.,
edge
Sn. D.
8 ad lib.
as fast as possible
black & white ab lib.
Glocksp. player goes back to Mar.
dim.

155
160
Picc.
Fl. 1 2
Ob. 1 2
E. H.
E♭ Cl.
B♭ Cl. 1 2 3
A. Cl.
B. Cl.
Bn. 1 2
A. Sax. 1 2
T. Sax.
Bar. Sax.
Bass Sax. Cb. Cl.
Tpt. 1 2 3 4
Hn. 1 2 3 4
Tbn. 1 2 3
Bar. 1 2
Tba.
Str. B. Cbn.
Timp.
Perc.
Mar.
Piano
Tutti
a2
1. p
2. fl. t.
p espressivo
senza vibrato (primitive, hollow sound)
Bass Sax. tacet until m 195
Harmon, stem in
p glissando
gliss.
mp glissando
Sus. Cym.
Large Gong
Mar. Large, soft mallets
mysterious, vibrating sound

Picc.
Fl. 1 2
Ob. 1 2
E. H.
E♭ Cl.
B♭ Cl. 1 2 3
A. Cl.
B. Cl.
Bn. 1 2
A. Sax. 1 2
T. Sax.
Bar. Sax.
Bass Sax. Cb. Cl.
Tpt. 1 2 3 4
Hn. 1 2 3 4
Tbn. 1 2 3
Bar. 1 2
Tba.
Str. B. Cbn.
Timp.
Mar.
Piano
fl. t.
165
gliss.
perd.
1. open
Mar. player goes to Xylophone

170
Picc.
Fl.
Ob.
E. H.
E♭ Cl.
B♭ Cl.
A. Cl.
B. Cl.
Bn.
A. Sax.
T. Sax.
Bar. Sax.
Bass Sax. Cb. Cl.
Tpt.
Hn.
Tbn.
Bar.
Tba.
Str. B. Cbn.
Timp.
Perc.
Vibr.
Xylo.
Piano
a2
mp espr.
p espr.
3. (mute)
2. open
Tutti
Str. B. arco a2
Sus. Cym.
L. V.

175
Picc.
Fl.
Ob.
E. H.
E♭ Cl.
B♭ Cl.
A. Cl.
B. Cl.
Bn.
A. Sax.
T. Sax.
Bar. Sax.
Bass Sax. Cb. Cl.
cresc. poco a poco
f espr.
mp cresc. poco a poco
dim.
poco a
poco
Tpt.
Hn.
Tbn.
Bar.
Tba.
Str. B. Cbn.
Timp.
Xylo.
Vibr.
Piano

180
Picc.
Fl. 1 2
Ob. 1 2
E. H.
E♭ Cl.
B♭ Cl. 1 2 3
A. Cl.
B. Cl.
Bn. 1 2
A. Sax. 1 2
T. Sax.
Bar. Sax.
Bass Sax. Cb. Cl.
180
Tpt. 1 2 3 4
stopped
Hn. 1 2 3 4
Tbn. 1 2 3
Bar. 1 2
Tba.
Str. B. Cbn.
Timp.
Xylo.
Vibr.
Piano

185
190
Picc.
Fl.
Ob.
E. H.
E♭ Cl.
B♭ Cl.
A. Cl.
B. Cl.
Bn.
A. Sax.
T. Sax.
Bar. Sax.
Bass Sax.
Cb. Cl.
Tpt.
Hn.
Tbn.
Bar.
Tba.
Str. B.
Cbn.
Timp.
Perc.
Xylo.
Vibr.
Piano
dim.
Cbn. tacet until m. 220
Str.B.
pizz.
Sus. Cym.
black
white

195
Picc.
Fl.
Ob.
E. H.
E♭ Cl.
B♭ Cl.
A. Cl.
B. Cl.
Bn.
A. Sax.
T. Sax.
Bar. Sax.
Bass Sax.
Cb. Cl.
Tpt.
Hn.
Tbn.
Bar.
Tba.
Str. B.
Cbn.
Timp.
Perc.
Xylo.
Vibr.
Piano
marc.
harsh, reedy
cresc.
a2
open
Str. B. arco
Sus. Cym.
S. D.
on the dome
hard mallets
sempre stacc.

200
Picc.
Fl.
Ob.
E. H.
1 ♭Cl.
B♭ Cl.
A. Cl.
B. Cl.
Bn.
A. Sax.
T. Sax.
Bar. Sax.
Bass Sax.
Cb. Cl.
Tpt.
Hn.
Tbn.
Bar.
Tba.
Str. B.
Cbn.
Timp.
Perc.
Xylo.
Vibr.
Piano
mp marc.
a2
nat.
mp cresc.
open
cresc.
Vibr.

Picc.
Fl. 1 2
Ob. 1 2
E. H.
E♭ Cl.
B♭ Cl. 1 2 3
A. Cl.
B. Cl.
Bn. 1 2
A. Sax. 1 2
T. Sax.
Bar. Sax.
Bass Sax. Cb. Cl.
Tpt. 1 2 3 4
Hn. 1 2 3 4
Tbn. 1 2 3
Bar. 1 2
Tba.
Str. B. Cbn.
Timp.
Perc.
Xylo.
Vibr.
Piano
205
a2
with S.D. Stick
Snares on
secco
(Ped. sim.)

210
Picc.
Fl. 1 2
Ob. 1 2
E. H.
E♭ Cl.
B♭ Cl. 1 2 3
A. Cl.
B. Cl.
Bn. 1 2
a2
A. Sax. 1 2
T. Sax.
8ad lib.
Bar. Sax.
Bass Sax. Cb. Cl.
cresc. poco a poco
f cresc. poco a poco
210
Tpt. 1 2 3 4
Hn. 1 2 3 4
Tbn. 1 2 3
Bar. 1 2
Tba.
Str. B. Cbn.
Timp.
mf
Perc.
Xylo.
Vibr.
(Ped.)
keep ped. on until 1st beat m.219
Piano

215
219
each player independently
Picc.
Fl.
Ob.
E. H.
E♭ Cl.
B♭ Cl.
A. Cl.
B. Cl.
Bn.
A. Sax.
T. Sax.
Bar. Sax.
Bass Sax. Cb. Cl.
Tpt.
Hn.
Tbn.
Bar.
Tba.
Str. B. Cbn.
Timp.
Sus. Cym.
S. D.
Xylo.
Vibr.
Piano
più f
sim. stacc.
gliss.
p cresc. poco a poco
mp molto cresc.
on black and white keys.
damp hard mallets
ca. 14

220
Picc.
Fl. 1 2
Ob. 1 2
E. H.
E♭ Cl.
B♭ Cl. 1 2 3
A. Cl.
B. Cl.
Bn. 1 2
A. Sax. 1 2
T. Sax.
Bar. Sax.
Bass Sax. Cb. Cl.
220
Tpt. 1 2 3 4
f molto espr.
Hn. 1 2 3 4
Tbn. 1 2 3
Bar. 1 2
Tba.
a2
Str. B. Cbn.
Timp.
gliss.
gl.
Sus. Cym. S. D.
L. V.
Xylo.
Vibr.
sim.
Piano

* 2nd Bass Cl. ad lib.

230
235 allarg.
Picc.
Fl. 1 2
Ob. 1 2
E. H.
E♭ Cl.
B♭ Cl. 1 2 3
A. Cl.
B. Cl.
Bn. 1 2
A. Sax. 1 2
T. Sax.
Bar. Sax.
Bass Sax. Cb. Cl.
Tpt. 1 2 3 4
Hn. 1 2 3 4
brassy
nat.
Tbn. 1 2 3
Bar. 1 2
ff
Tba.
più f
Str. B. Cbn.
Timp.
quasi trem.
S. D.
approx speed here
f
Sus. Cym.
p
cresc.
Xylo.
Vibr.
Piano
accel. into tremolo
mf
cresc. poco a poco

* If two Trombones 3 available one will play octave higher (col. Tbns, 1 and 2.) until m. 246.

* * If not enough time, omit m. 242, but play m. 244.

Picc.
Fl. 1 2
Ob. 1 2
E. H.
E♭Cl.
B♭Cl. 1 2 3
A. Cl.
B. Cl.
Bn. 1 2
A. Sax. 1 2
T. Sax.
Bar. Sax.
Bass Sax. Cb. Cl.
Tpt. 1 2 3 4
Hn. 1 2 3 4
Tbn. 1 2 3
Bar. 1 2
Tba.
Str. B. Cbn.
Timp.
Perc.
Vibr.
Mar.
Piano
245
Molto rit.
ff
sim.
cresc.
St.B
Cbn.
G.
B.D.
B.Dr.
S.D.
f
sf
p
cresc. molto

* As high as D if possible.

255
260
Picc.
Fl. 1 2
Ob. 1 2
E. H.
E♭ Cl.
B♭ Cl. 1 2 3
A. Cl.
B. Cl.
Bn. 1 2
a2
f espr.
dim.
A. Sax. 1 2
T. Sax.
Bar. Sax.
Bass Sax. Cb. Cl.
Tpt. 1 2 3 4
f marc. straight mute dim.
Hn. 1 2 3 4
gliss.
gl.
espr.
f marc. stopped, brassy dim.
poco a poco
Tbn. 1 2 3
Bar. 1 2
Tba.
Str. B. Cbn.
hard felt sticks
Timp.
mf
slow glissando
Perc.
B.D.
Mar.
soft mallets
Vibr.
damp
Piano

265
Picc.
Fl. 1 2
Ob. 1 2
E. H.
E♭ Cl.
B♭ Cl. 1 2 3
A. Cl.
B. Cl.
Bn. 1 2
A. Sax. 1 2
T. Sax.
Bar. Sax.
Bass Sax. Cb. Cl.
Tpt. 1 2 3 4
Hn. 1 2 3 4
Tbn. 1 2 3
Bar. 1 2
Tba.
Str. B. Cbn.
Timp.
Perc.
Vibr.
Mar.
Piano
1. Solo
mf espr.
mf cantabile
dim.
mp tranquillo
mf dim. poco a poco
mp dim.
sim.
a2
Solo
Str. B. pizz.
Medium soft sticks on the dome
Small Sus. Cym.
motor on medium speed
soft mallets
poco a poco
f poco espr.

* Lip pressure and release (notation approx).

Conductor: The sound of the entire clarinet section must disappear progressively. Keep the fermatas as long as necessary, without rushing. Then keep a moment of silence.

* See preceding Cl. 1 solo.

** If E♭ Key available, up to $\frac{1}{3}$ of all Cls. should play the lower E♭.

0 73999 44610 4
HL50244610

Associated Music Publishers, Inc.
Distributed By
HAL•LEONARD®

ISBN 978-0-634-01353-9
9 780634 013539